CONTENTS

THE SECOND WORLD WAR

The Second World War was fought by many countries around the world. It lasted six years, from 1939 to 1945.

Battles in the Second World War were fought on land, at sea and in the sky.

The UK, France, the Soviet Union and the **USA** were on one side of the war. They were called the **Allies**. The Allies fought against Germany, Italy and Japan.

Winston Churchill was the leader of the UK for most of the Second World War. He felt certain that the Allies would win.

FACT CAT FACT

Sixty **million** people died in the Second World War. Most of them, around 40 million people, were ordinary people, not soldiers.

THE WAR STARTS

In 1933, a man named Adolf Hitler became the leader of Germany. Hitler wanted to make Germany more powerful.

Hitler and his **followers** were known as the Nazis. The Nazi symbol was a swastika.

swastika

Hitler wanted to control more land in **Europe**. In 1939, Germany **invaded** Poland. The UK and France had promised to **defend** Poland. So, in September 1939, they went to war with Germany.

Hitler and the Nazi Party didn't like **Jewish** people. In Nazi Germany, Jewish people had to live in special areas. They had to wear a special symbol that showed that they were Jewish. What was the symbol?

German soldiers invaded Poland in September 1939.

AROUND THE WORLD

At first, the battles in the Second World War were fought in Europe. Germany invaded France and Belgium in 1940. There weren't enough Allied soldiers in France to stop them.

After the Germans invaded France, many Allied soldiers were trapped on the beaches of northern France. They were rescued in boats and taken to Britain.

Later, the fighting spread to the Soviet Union, Africa and Asia. In 1941, Japan attacked US battleships in Pearl Harbor, Hawaii. After this, the USA joined the war on the Allied side.

The Japanese airforce dropped bombs on US ships during the attack on Pearl Harbor. What is a harbour?

FACT CAT FACT

Over 2,400 US soldiers were killed in the Pearl Harbor attack.

WEAPONS

During the Second World War, people made new powerful weapons. They made tanks from thick metal to **protect** the soldiers inside.

This American tank from the Second World War had a powerful gun.

People made aeroplanes for different jobs. Large aeroplanes carried and dropped bombs. Small, fast aeroplanes fought each other in the sky and **spied** on the enemy.

These large aeroplanes from the USA are dropping bombs on Japan.

FACT CAT FACT

The German army used flying bombs, powered by their own jet engines. They could find their own way to the **target**.

BOMBING CITIES

Both sides dropped bombs on cities. The bombs **destroyed** houses and buildings. Many ordinary people were **injured** and killed.

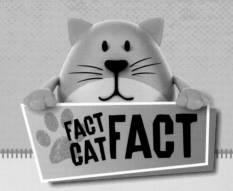

In the evenings, there was a **blackout**. People had to turn the lights off in their houses and on the streets. This made it harder for enemy aeroplanes to see them and drop bombs on them.

London was hit by many bombs during the Second World War. Find out the name of another city that was bombed.

People in Britain built **shelters** in their gardens. They went into the shelters when bombs started to fall.

In Britain, children that lived in cities were sent to stay in the countryside. There were fewer bomb attacks in the countryside.

AT HOME

Ordinary people at home worked hard to help their country win the war. Women worked on farms to grow extra food. They also made weapons and vehicles in factories.

This woman is working as a mechanic in the USA. She is building an aeroplane.

There was less food to go around during the Second World War. It was hard for ships to bring food to countries. Food was **rationed** in many European countries. People could only buy a certain amount of some foods each week.

These are some of the weekly rations for one person in Britain. Why couldn't people eat bananas in Britain during the war?

1 egg

225g of sugar

four slices of bacon

60g cheese

FACT CAT **FACT**

Petrol, soap and clothes were also rationed in Britain during and after the war.

THE HOLOCAUST

During the Second World War, the Nazis started treating Jewish people very badly. Some Jewish people moved to other countries. The Jewish people that couldn't leave tried to hide from the Nazis.

nederland
ANNE FRANK
60c

Anne Frank was a Jewish girl who tried to hide from the Nazis in the Netherlands. She kept a diary about her life.

The Nazis sent many Jewish people to work in camps. Only the strongest people were allowed to work. The Nazis killed the other Jewish people with **poison gas**. This is known as the **Holocaust**.

Jewish people in the camps had to wear a striped uniform.

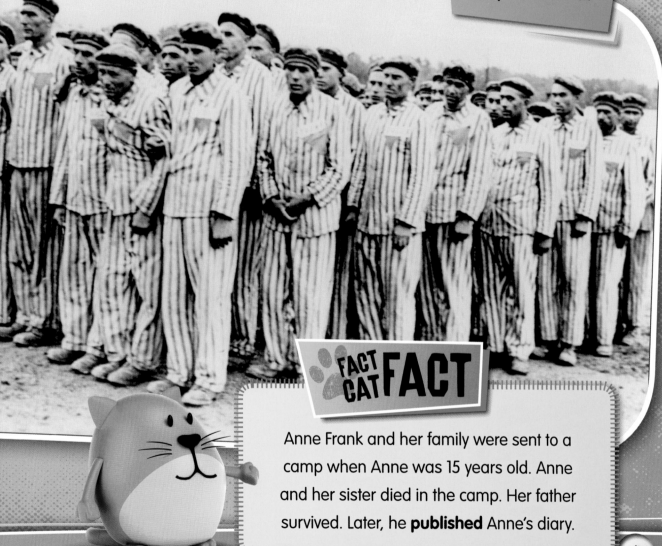

FACT CAT FACT

Anne Frank and her family were sent to a camp when Anne was 15 years old. Anne and her sister died in the camp. Her father survived. Later, he **published** Anne's diary.

THE WAR ENDS

Slowly, the Allies started to take back land in Europe from the Nazis. On 8 May 1945, Germany **surrendered**. The Second World War had ended in Europe.

People around the world celebrated the end of the war on 8 May. Why is this day known as VE Day?

The war against Japan continued. In August 1945, the USA dropped **atomic bombs** on two cities in Japan. After this, Japan surrendered. The Second World War was over.

The atomic bombs created huge explosions. They destroyed many buildings and killed hundreds of thousands of people.

FACT CAT FACT

The atomic bomb is the most destructive weapon ever invented. No one has used atomic bombs as a weapon since the Second World War.

REMEMBERING THE WAR

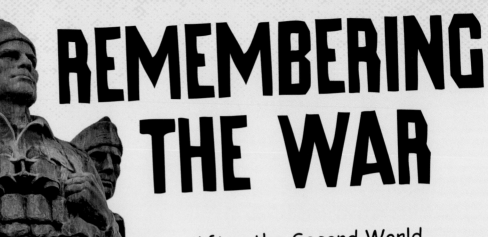

After the Second World War, people had to rebuild many towns and cities. They built memorials to **honour** and remember the people who died in the war.

This Scottish monument helps us to remember the soldiers that died in the war.

UNITED · WE · CONQUER

Every year, we remember the Second World War on 11 November. This day is known as **Remembrance Day**. On this day, we also remember the people who died in the First World War and other wars.

The Second World War killed more people and damaged more places than any other war in history.

Soldiers take part in processions on Remembrance Day. Many people wear poppies on Remembrance Day.

poppies

QUIZ

Try to answer the questions below. Look back through the book to help you. Check your answers on page 24.

1 When did the Second World War begin?

a) 1914

b) 1925

c) 1939

2 Germany fought on the same side as the UK. True or not true?

a) true

b) not true

3 Why did people turn off their lights at night?

a) to hide from enemy planes

b) to save electricity

c) to get enough sleep

4 Eggs were rationed during the war. True or not true?

a) true

b) not true

5 When did the war end in Europe?

a) May 1945

b) August 1945

c) December 1945

6 The USA dropped atomic bombs on Japan. True or not true?

a) true

b) not true

GLOSSARY

Allies the armies of Britain, France, the Soviet Union and later, the USA, that fought on the same side

atomic bomb a very powerful bomb

blackout a time in the evenings during the Second World War when lights were turned off to help prevent air raids

defend to protect someone or something from being attacked

destroy to damage something so badly that it doesn't exist any more

Europe the continent that includes the countries of France, Germany, the UK and many more countries

follower someone who agrees with and supports a leader

Holocaust the murder of millions of people during the Second World War by the Nazis. Most of these people were Jewish

honour to show that you think someone or something is important

injured hurt

invade to enter a country and use force to take control of it

Jewish a Jewish person follows the religion of Judaism

million one thousand thousand (1,000,000)

poison gas gas that will hurt or kill you if you breathe it in

protect to keep someone or something safe

publish to print copies of a book so that other people can read it

ration to limit the amount of something that people can have

Remembrance Day an event on 11 November in which people remember and pay respect to those who died in wars throughout history

shelter a place that protects you from danger

spy to secretly try to get information

surrender to stop fighting and say that you have lost

target a place or object at which bombs or bullets are aimed

USA the United States of America

INDEX

ANSWERS

Pages 4–20

Page 7: A yellow star

Page 9: A harbour is an area of water where ships can shelter

Page 12: Some cities include Coventry, Belfast, Dresden and Cologne.

Page 15: Because bananas can't be grown in Britain and it was difficult for ships to bring them to Britain.

Page 18: VE stands for Victory in Europe.

Quiz answers

1   c - 1939
2   not true – the UK fought against Germany
3   a – to hide from enemy planes
4   true
5   a – May 1945
6   true

FACT CAT

THE SECOND WORLD WAR

Izzi Howell

FACT CAT

Get your paws on this fantastic new mega-series from Wayland!

Join our Fact Cat on a journey of fun learning about every subject under the sun!

Published in paperback in Great Britain in 2020 by Wayland
Copyright © Hodder and Stoughton, 2017

ISBN: 978 1 5263 0607 4

10 9 8 7 6 5 4 3 2 1

MIX
Paper from responsible sources
FSC® C104740

Wayland
An imprint of Hachette Children's Group
Part of Hodder & Stoughton
Carmelite House
50 Victoria Embankment
London EC4Y 0DZ

An Hachette UK Company
www.hachette.co.uk
www.hachettechildrens.co.uk

A catalogue for this title is available from the British Library
Printed and bound in Dubai
Produced for Wayland by
White-Thomson Publishing Ltd
www.wtpub.co.uk

Editor: Izzi Howell
Design: Clare Nicholas
Fact Cat illustrations: Shutterstock/Julien Troneur
Consultant: Karina Philip

Picture and illustration credits:
Alamy: World History Archive cover, Trinity Mirror/Mirrorpix 13; Getty: IWM 8, © Hulton-Deutsch Collection/CORBIS/Corbis via Getty Images 18; Shutterstock: Everett Historical title page, 4, 7, 9, 10, 11, 12, 14, 17 and 19, Olga Popova 5, Elzbieta Sekowska 6, Coprid 15tl, Abramova Elena 15tr, Nattika 15bl, Hong vo 15br, Tony Baggett 16, Ulmus Media 20, Bikeworldtravel 21t, Ed Samuel 21b.
Should there be any inadvertent omission, please apply to the publisher for rectification.

The author, Izzi Howell, is a writer and editor specialising in children's educational publishing.

The consultant, Karina Philip, is a teacher and a primary literacy consultant with an MA in creative writing.

FACT CAT FACT

There is a question for you to answer on most spreads in this book. You can check your answers on page 24.